SUPER
SANDCASTLE:
Creature Features

What Has Claws?

Mary Elizabeth Salzmann

ABDO
Publishing Company

Published by ABDO Publishing Company, 8000 West 78th Street, Edina, Minnesota 55439. Copyright © 2008 by Abdo Consulting Group, Inc. International copyrights reserved in all countries. No part of this book may be reproduced in any form without written permission from the publisher. Super SandCastle™ is a trademark and logo of ABDO Publishing Company.

Printed in the United States.

Credits
Editor: Pam Price
Content Developer: Nancy Tuminelly
Cover and Interior Design and Production: Mighty Media
Photo Credits: Eyewire, iStockphoto (Denis Tabler, Torsten Wittmann), Shutterstock, Steve Wewerka

Library of Congress Cataloging-in-Publication Data

Salzmann, Mary Elizabeth, 1968-

  What has claws? / Mary Elizabeth Salzmann.

    p. cm. -- (Creature features)

  ISBN 978-1-59928-865-9

  1. Claws--Juvenile literature. I. Title.

  QL942.S247 2008

  591.47--dc22

                    2007005648

Super SandCastle™ books are created by a team of professional educators, reading specialists, and content developers around five essential components—phonemic awareness, phonics, vocabulary, text comprehension, and fluency—to assist young readers as they develop reading skills and strategies and increase their general knowledge. All books are written, reviewed, and leveled for guided reading, early reading intervention, and Accelerated Reader® programs for use in shared, guided, and independent reading and writing activities to support a balanced approach to literacy instruction.

About SUPER SANDCASTLE™

Bigger Books for Emerging Readers
Grades PreK–3

Created for library, classroom, and at-home use, Super SandCastle™ books support and engage young readers as they develop and build literacy skills and will increase their general knowledge about the world around them. Super SandCastle™ books are part of SandCastle™, the leading PreK–3 imprint for emerging and beginning readers. Super SandCastle™ features a larger trim size for more reading fun.

Let Us Know
Super SandCastle™ would like to hear your stories about reading this book. What was your favorite page? Was there something hard that you needed help with? Share the ups and downs of learning to read. We want to hear from you! Send us an e-mail.

sandcastle@abdopublishing.com

Contact us for a complete list of SandCastle™, Super SandCastle™, and other nonfiction and fiction titles from ABDO Publishing Company.

www.abdopublishing.com • 8000 West 78th Street
Edina, MN 55439 • 800-800-1312 • 952-831-1632 fax

Claws are the sharp nails on an animal's toes.
The pincers of sea animals are also called claws.

4

Cats have claws.

When cats relax, they retract their claws. Cats extend their claws for hunting, defense, climbing, kneading, or traction.

Bears have claws.

Brown bear claws can be up to six inches long. Bears use their claws mostly for digging.

Hawks have claws.

Hawk claws are also called talons.
Hawks swoop down and grab their
prey off the ground with their claws.

Lobsters have claws.

A lobster's claws are also called pincers. If a lobster's claw gets trapped or grabbed, it will fall off. The lobster will grow a new one.

Badgers have claws.

A badger's front claws are longer than its back claws. Badgers use their claws to dig tunnels.

Komodo dragons have claws.

Until they are about four years old, Komodo dragons use their claws to climb trees. Then they become too big to climb trees and spend the rest of their lives on the ground.

Armadillos have claws.

Armadillos use their claws to dig in the ground for insects and grubs to eat. They also dig dens for shelter.

Sloths have claws.

Sloths have long, curved claws that allow them to easily hang on to tree branches. Sloths spend nearly their entire lives in trees.

Kangaroos have claws.

Kangaroos use their claws as weapons for fighting and defending themselves.

What would you do if you had claws?